The Official
Portsmouth
Football Club
Annual 2008

Written By Eleanor Frost

A Grange Publication

© 2007. Published by Grange Communications Ltd., Edinburgh, under licence from Portsmouth Football Club. Printed in the EU.

ISBN 978-1-905426-91-1

Photographs © Joe Pepler/Portsmouth Football Club.

£6.99

Contents

To Adam,
Happy 11th birthday!
From Jake

Manager's Message

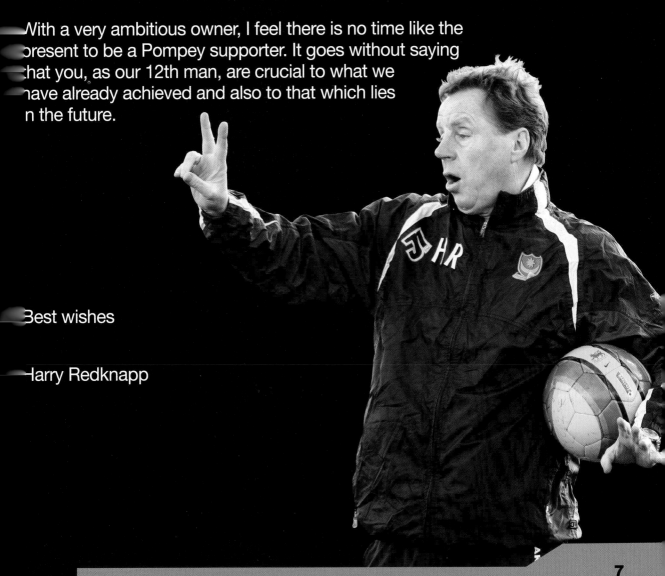

t's been a wonderful season at Fratton Park and we all feel privileged to have been part of the most successful performing team since the mid 1950s. Having been a football crazy kid at that time I certainly know what an act that was to follow!

t goes without saying that I am delighted for our supporters who, given the lack of success at the club in over half a century, have always believed their team can play at the highest level. Several generations of fans could only previously listen to stories of the good old days, but I would like to think that now a new generation will have their own great tales to tell.

We have seen immense performances from players like Sol Campbell, David James, Linvoy Primus, Matthew Taylor and Kanu to name just a few. And with the additions that we have already made this season, the future is looking very good for the club.

With a very ambitious owner, I feel there is no time like the present to be a Pompey supporter. It goes without saying that you, as our 12th man, are crucial to what we have already achieved and also to that which lies n the future.

Best wishes

Harry Redknapp

August

A new look team emerged from the tunnel at Fratton Park on a sunny August afternoon to kick off the 2006/07 campaign. Heralding a new dawn and lofty ambitions, the side contained England internationals Sol Campbell and David James. Other notable additions in August included Nigerian striker Kanu, Andrew Cole and rising stars Glen Johnson and Niko Kranjcar – among others.

A thrilling 3-0 opener against Blackburn laid down Pompey's intentions for the season. Svetoslav Todorov started

proceedings in style with Pompey's first goal. Coming on as a substitute, Kanu silenced his doubters by adding two more, though a missed penalty denied him a hat-trick on his debut.

After the goalscoring exploits of the weekend, a midweek visit to Manchester City followed. It was a dour 0-0 stalemate and was overshadowed by the horrific incident which saw Pedro Mendes carried from the pitch and taken to hospital after being poleaxed by Ben Thatcher. The challenge was universally condemned by fans, experts and players alike and the defender was eventually handed a lengthy ban.

However the month ended on a high with a phenomenal 4-0 win at the Riverside Stadium. Once again Kanu was in magnificent form, bagging another brace for his new club. Benjani Mwaruwari netted his first of the season, while Todorov rounded off the match in style.

results

Home	Goals	
Portsmouth	3-0	Blackburn
Todorov 26		
Kanu 62, 84		
Manchester City	0-0	Portsmouth
Middlesbrough	0-4	Portsmouth
		Kanu 7, 57
		Benjani 50
		Todorov 90

September

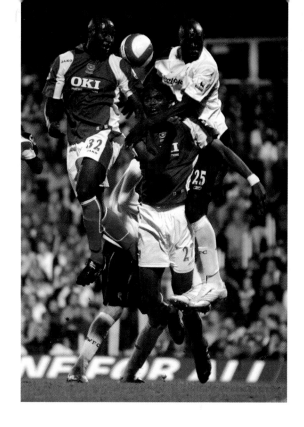

Portsmouth continued to exceed expectations going into September. Benjani celebrated his first goal in front of the home crowd during the 1-0 win over Wigan - coincidentally the same team that he had scored his debut strike against during that crucial game at the JJB Stadium in April 2006.

Another 1-0 victory followed, this time at The Valley and it was another of Pompey's African stars who led the celebrations, as Lomana LuaLua put away the winning shot from a Sean Davis cross. That result sent Pompey to the top of the table for the ensuing week.

The first defeat of the season came on an emotional night at Fratton Park at the end of the month, as Milan Mandaric attended his final game as Chairman. Despite playing some fantastic football, luck seemed to be against Pompey's strike force. They were left frustrated at being unable to breach the Bolton defence. The match was the team's first loss of the season after they conceded their first league goal of the campaign.

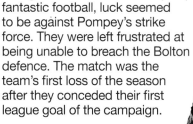

In other competitions, Portsmouth progressed to the next round of the League Cup after beating Mansfield Town 2-1 at Field Mill.

Benjani celebrated his first goal in front of the home crowd

results

Home	Goals	
Portsmouth	1-0	Wigan Athletic
Benjani 49		
Charlton Athletic	0-1	Portsmouth
		LuaLua 74
Mansfield Town	1-2	Portsmouth *
		Fernandes 5
* *League Cup*		Taylor 33
Portsmouth	0-1	Bolton Wanderers

October

The month got off to a disappointing start against Tottenham when the team were beaten 2-1 at White Hart Lane amid controversy after the London side was awarded a decisive penalty; however television coverage proved that Mendes had not touched Didier Zakora.

The defeat was compounded by another away loss in the capital, this time to Chelsea although Benjani was able to pull a goal back for Portsmouth at Stamford Bridge.

However, resounding home wins against West Ham (2-0) and Reading (3-1) kept spirits high. Notably Andrew Cole broke his duck for Pompey against the Hammers after displaying some neat footwork to stay on his feet before he tucked the ball home. Against the Royals it was time to dust off the Rocket-Man accolades for Pedro Mendes, who unleashed one of his super strikes to secure the three points for the Blues.

Away from the Premiership, Portsmouth exited the League Cup in farcical weather conditions at Newcastle as the match, which was played in torrential rain, ended 3-0 in the hosts' favour.

results

Home	Goals	
Tottenham Hotspur	2-1	Portsmouth
		Kanu 40
Portsmouth	2-0	West Ham United
Kanu 24		
Cole 82		
Chelsea	2-1	Portsmouth
		Mwaruwari 69
Newcastle	3-0	Portsmouth*
		League Cup
Portsmouth	3-1	Reading
Gunnarsson 10 og		
Kanu 52		
Mendes 66		

November

As winter descended on the South Coast, November proved to be a mixed month for Portsmouth in terms of both results and performances.

It began with a 3-0 defeat at Old Trafford as an injury-hit Pompey did well to keep the attacking prowess of Manchester United at bay. The following week, an inspired performance from Fulham's Antti Niemi at Fratton Park prevented Pompey from claiming all three points as, despite throwing everything at the visiting team, only Andrew Cole was able to find a way past the Finnish 'keeper.

Seven days later LuaLua scored from a last minute penalty against newly-promoted Watford to beat them 2-1 at Fratton Park.

The month closed with two tough matches in four days. A disappointing defeat at St James' Park was followed by a gritty display at Liverpool to earn a 0-0 draw as the Blues became only the second team of the season to leave Anfield with a point and the first to deny them a goal in front of the Kop.

results

A mixed month for Portsmouth in terms of both results and performances.

Home	Goals	
Manchester United	3-0	Portsmouth
Portsmouth	1-1	Fulham
Cole 74		
Portsmouth	2-1	Watford
Kanu 44		
LuaLua 89 pen		
Newcastle	1-0	Portsmouth
Liverpool	0-0	Portsmouth

December

The final month of 2006 belonged to just one player at Fratton Park – a certain Matthew Taylor, whose goalscoring exploits hit headlines and wowed supporters and experts alike.

The 25-year-old racked up five goals in quick succession, starting with a brace against Aston Villa at home on the 2nd.

Just seven days later, Taylor then unleashed a phenomenal shot from around forty-yards out. Fratton Park rocked as his audacious volley soared and then dipped past an astonished Tim Howard and into the waiting Everton goal. Kanu scored the second in the 2-0 win, itself a stunning strike, but the plaudits deservedly belonged to the young Englishman.

Pompey's first ever visit to the Emirates Stadium saw them earn a

results

Home	Goals	
Portsmouth	2-2	Aston Villa
Taylor 52, 80 pen		
Portsmouth	2-0	Everton
Taylor 14		
Kanu 26		
Arsenal	2-2	Portsmouth
		Pamarot 45
		Taylor 47
Portsmouth	3-1	Sheffield United
Kozluk 48 og		
Campbell 54		
Pamarot 68		
West Ham United	1-2	Portsmouth
		Primus 16, 38
Bolton Wanderers	3-2	Portsmouth
		Taylor 2
		Cole 89

superb 2-2 draw, with Taylor yet again grabbing another great goal. That same game also witnessed Noé Pamarot's name on the score sheet for Portsmouth for the first time.

An emphatic 3-1 home win over Sheffield United was marked by Sol Campbell scoring his first for Pompey. Then a 2-1 Boxing Day win at West Ham rounded off a fantastic Christmas for the team. Incidentally, the goals came from Linvoy Primus, scoring for the first time since 26 December 2004.

The year was rounded off with a visit to Bolton. Although the team suffered defeat at the Reebok Stadium, they finished the year on 35 points - just three less than they had at the end of the previous season.

January

The first league game of 2007, on New Year's Day, saw Pompey earn a hard fought point against Tottenham at Fratton Park. Benjani provided Pompey's only goal, after linking up with a Niko Kranjcar pass.

That result was echoed at Sheffield United's Bramall Lane ground just under a fortnight later, only this time it was Gary O'Neil's name on the score sheet as he claimed his first of the season and in doing so he was finally able to have a haircut, having made a pre-season bet with Sean Davis that meant neither could cut their tresses until one of them scored.

Pompey then slipped to a shock defeat at the hands of relegation-threatened Charlton at Fratton Park and concluded the month with a scoreless draw at home against Middlesbrough.

January also saw the beginning and the end of the team's FA Cup run. It started with a home tie against Wigan when an injury time winner from Kanu prevented the game going to a replay at the JJB Stadium. The next round pitted Pompey against Manchester United at Old Trafford, where a brace from substitute Wayne Rooney sealed Pompey's fate.

Away from the match action, the transfer window allowed Portsmouth to pull off a real coup by signing Arsenal's Lauren ahead of a number of other interested clubs. The two other January additions were Djimi Traoré from Charlton and Arnold Mvuemba, who joined on loan from French side Rennes.

results

Home	Goals	
Portsmouth	1-1	Tottenham Hotspur
Benjani 29		
Portsmouth	2-1	Wigan Athletic *
Cole 64		
Kanu 90		*FA Cup
Sheffield United	1-1	Portsmouth
		O'Neil 81
Portsmouth	0-1	Charlton
Manchester United	2-1	Portsmouth*
*FA Cup		Kanu 87
Portsmouth	0-0	Middlesbrough

February

Disappointment is perhaps the key word for the first and last games of February.

An uninspired performance witnessed the team slip to a 1-0 defeat at Wigan's JJB Stadium on the 3rd. However, Pompey shook off the loss and bounced back at home in the best way possible with a fantastic result against Manchester City.

Once again Pedro Mendes hit the headlines against the Mancunian team after curling in a fantastic strike against Stuart Pearce's side. It was reminiscent of the two he scored against the same opposition which sparked the previous season's 'Great Escape'. Barely 30 minutes after hitting the net, a late tackle from Joey Barton saw the Portuguese midfielder carried off the pitch.

The third game for the south coast side this month proved to be a frustrating one for the team as a visit to Ewood Park spelled a 3-0 defeat in a reversal of the opening match of the season.

results

Home	Goals	
Wigan Athletic	1-0	Portsmouth
Portsmouth	2-1	Manchester City
Mendes 5		
Kanu 81		
Blackburn	3-0	Portsmouth

Pedro Mendes hit the headlines against the Mancunian team after curling in a fantastic strike

March

Spring kicked off with a tough visit from Chelsea the day after manager Harry Redknapp's 60th birthday. It ended in the opposition's favour, although Pompey put in a great performance and it was only the brilliance of Petr Cech that kept the side from getting anything from the game.

Away draws at Reading and Fulham kept momentum going though, as the push for Europe continued. But the point at Craven Cottage had an air of dissatisfaction to it as an injury time strike that allowed Fulham to draw level after Pompey went ahead thanks to a stylish Niko Kranjcar effort, which swept into the net from just outside the area in the opening minutes of the game.

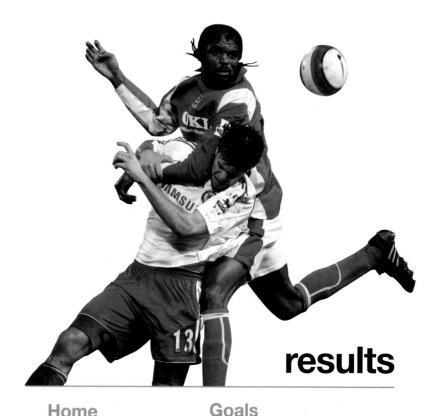

Pompey went ahead thanks to a stylish Niko Kranjcar effort, which swept into the net from just outside the area

results

Home	Goals	
Portsmouth	0-2	Chelsea
Reading	0-0	Portsmouth
Fulham	1-1	Portsmouth
		Kranjcar 4

April

April started with Pompey stunning the league leaders with a 2-1 victory when Manchester United arrived at Fratton Park. Once again it was Matthew Taylor who rose to the occasion to hit the net, although a comical own goal from Rio Ferdinand in the dying minutes sealed the win for Portsmouth.

However the elation would be short-lived, as just two days after beating the top-placed side there was disappointment at Vicarage Road. A 4-2 defeat at the hands of the bottom team ensured that the team's feet would stay well and truly on the ground.

However, this proved to be merely a blip in an otherwise successful month. Back on home turf, Pompey saw off challenges from Newcastle and Liverpool, both games ending in 2-1 wins.

The month concluded with a visit to Villa Park on a drab Sunday afternoon. The match itself was an uneventful one, but it will be certain to get a mention in the history books as the game in which the long-standing Premier League clean-sheet record, previously held by Arsenal legend David Seaman, was beaten by David James – against one of his former sides no less!

Off the pitch, the club topped the month off when it revealed plans for a dazzling new waterfront stadium. However, alongside the celebrations there was also sadness, as former Pompey manager and England World Cup hero Alan Ball passed away aged just 61.

results

Home	Goals	
Portsmouth	2-1	Manchester United
Taylor 30		
Ferdinand 89 Og		
Watford	4-2	Portsmouth
		Taylor 16
		Mvuemba 81
Portsmouth	2-1	Newcastle
Benjani 7		
Taylor 59		
Aston Villa	0-0	Portsmouth
Portsmouth	2-1	Liverpool
Benjani 27		
Kranjcar 32		

May

The final two games of the season brought mixed emotions to the Fratton Park stands. A 3-0 loss at Goodison Park meant that Pompey's European hopes would hang on the last game of the season.

However, a controversial decision by the retiring referee Graham Poll to rule out Niko Kranjcar's effort against Arsenal saw the match finish goalless and ended Portsmouth's interest in the UEFA Cup. However, there was much to celebrate.

In finishing in ninth spot in the league, Pompey not only had their highest Premier League placing since their promotion in 2003, that means it was also the club's top finish in more than 50 years. An impressive achievement indeed, and Pompey fans can look back over the past 2006/07 season with an immense amount of pride.

Pompey's European hopes would hang on the last game of the season.

results

home		goals	
Everton		3-0	Portsmouth
Portsmouth		0-0	Arsenal

Season Statistics

Appearances and Goals

Name	DoB	PL	LGC	FAC	TOT	Gls	YC	RC
Sol Campbell	18.09.74	32	0	2	34	1	1	0
Andrew Cole	15.10.71	5(13)	2	2	9(13)	4	1	0
Sean Davis	20.09.79	29(2)	1	1	31(2)	0	6	0
Roudolphe Douala	25.09.78	1(6)	0(2)	0(1)	1(9)	0	0	0
Richard Duffy	30.08.85	0	1	0	1	0	0	0
Manuel Fernandes	05.02.86	7(3)	2	0	9(3)	1	1	0
Richard Hughes	25.06.79	11(7)	1(1)	1	13(8)	0	5	0
David James	01.08.70	38	1	2	41	0	2	0
Glen Johnson	23.08.84	25(1)	0	2	27(1)	0	4	0
Nwankwo Kanu	01.08.76	32(4)	0	0(2)	32(6)	12	3	0
Dean Kiely	10.10.70	0	1	0	1	0	0	0
Ognijen Koroman	19.09.78	0(1)	1(1)	0	1(2)	0	0	0
Niko Kranjcar	13.08.84	11(13)	2	2	15(13)	2	1	0
Lauren	19.01.77	9(1)	0	1	10(1)	0	1	0
Lomana Tresor LuaLua	28.12.80	8(14)	2	0	10(14)	2	0	0
Pedro Mendes	26.02.79	25(1)	0	2	27(1)	2	3	1
Arnold Mvuemba	28.01.85	1(6)	0	0	1(6)	1	1	0
Benjani Mwaruwari	13.08.78	25(6)	0(1)	1(1)	26(8)	6	0	0
Andrew O'Brien	29.06.79	1(2)	2	0	3(2)	0	0	0
Gary O'Neil	18.05.83	35	0	2	37	1	7	0
Noe Pamarot	14.04.79	21(2)	2	0	23(2)	2	5	0
Linvoy Primus	14.09.73	36	1	2	39	2	1	0
Dejan Stefanovic	28.10.74	20	0	0	20	0	4	0
Matthew Taylor	27.11.81	30(5)	2	2	34(5)	9	4	0
David Thompson	12.09.77	5(7)	1(1)	0(1)	6(9)	0	4	0
Svetoslav Todorov	30.08.78	1(3)	0	0	1(3)	2	1	0
Djimi Traore	01.03.80	10	0	0	10	0	0	0

Pompey's Attendance Records 2006/07

Highest (H):	20,223 v Manchester United	(7 April 2007)
Highest (A):	76,004 v Manchester United	(4 November 2006)
Lowest (H):	14,336 v Wigan Athletic - FA Cup	(6 January 2007)
Lowest (A):	6,646 v Mansfield Town - League Cup	(19 September 2006)
Average (H):	19,586	
Average (A):	34,212	

Pompey's Goalscoring Records 2006/07

Biggest home win	Portsmouth 3 - 0 Blackburn	(19 August 2006)
Biggest home defeat	Portsmouth 0 - 2 Chelsea	(3 March 2007)
Biggest away win	Middlesbrough 0 - 4 Portsmouth	(28 August 2006)
Biggest away defeat	Newcastle 3 - 0 Portsmouth - League Cup	(25 October 2006)
	Manchester United 3 - 0 Portsmouth	(4 November 2006)
	Blackburn 3 - 0 Portsmouth	(25 February 2007)
	Everton 3 - 0 Portsmouth	(5 May 2007)

Goals Scored By Game

0 Goals	15
1 Goal	9
2 Goals	14
3 Goals	3
4 Goals	1

Goals Conceded By Game

0 Goals	12
1 Goal	18
2 Goals	6
3 Goals	5
4 Goals	1

2006/07 League Table

	P	Home					Away					GD	PT
		W	D	L	F	A	W	D	L	F	A		
Man Utd	38	15	2	2	46	12	13	3	3	37	15	56	89
Chelsea	38	12	7	0	37	11	12	4	3	27	13	40	83
Liverpool	38	14	4	1	39	7	6	4	9	18	20	30	68
Arsenal	38	12	6	1	43	16	7	5	7	20	19	28	68
Tottenham	38	12	3	4	34	22	5	6	8	23	32	3	60
Everton	38	11	4	4	33	17	4	9	6	19	19	16	58
Bolton	38	9	5	5	26	20	7	3	9	21	32	-5	56
Reading	38	11	2	6	29	20	5	5	9	23	27	5	55
PORTSMOUTH	38	11	5	3	28	15	3	7	9	17	27	3	54
Blackburn	38	9	3	7	31	25	6	4	9	21	29	-2	52
Aston Villa	38	7	8	4	20	14	4	9	6	23	27	2	50
Middlesbrough	38	10	3	6	31	24	2	7	10	13	25	-5	46
Newcastle	38	7	7	5	23	20	4	3	12	15	27	-9	43
Man City	38	5	6	8	10	16	6	3	10	19	28	-15	42
West Ham	38	8	2	9	24	26	4	3	12	11	33	-24	41
Fulham	38	7	7	5	18	18	1	8	10	20	42	-22	39
Wigan	38	5	4	10	18	30	5	4	10	19	29	-22	38
Sheffield United	38	7	6	6	24	21	3	2	14	8	34	-23	38
Charlton	38	7	5	7	19	20	1	5	13	15	40	-26	34
Watford	38	3	9	7	19	25	2	4	13	10	4	-30	28

What do you remember about the 2006/07 season?

1   Who scored Pompey's first goal of the 2006/07 campaign?

2   And who scored the last?

3   How many clean sheets did Pompey keep?
A) 6, B) 12 or C) 18

4   In which game did Kanu make his first Pompey start?

5   Which team did Pompey sign Niko Kranjcar from?

6   Which side did Pompey beat 2-1 at Fratton Park to progress to the fourth round of the FA Cup?

7   Who was Pompey's top scorer in 2006/2007?

8   And what was his tally (including league and cup goals)?

9   Which defender scored his first goal for Pompey against Arsenal at the Emirates Stadium on 16 December 2006?

10 David James broke the Premiership clean sheet record against Aston Villa on April 22 2007. How many had he kept at the end of that game to claim the accolade?

11 How many league games did Pompey draw?
A) 12, B) 15 or C) 18

12 Where did Pompey finish in the league standings?

Answers on page 60

See how much you know about Portsmouth past and present...

1. In which year was Portsmouth Football Club founded?

   A) 1898, B) 1918 or C) 1938

2. Sir Arthur Conan Doyle played for Pompey in the club's early days. Which famous detective did he create?

3. As well as his long-range goal against Everton in December 2006, Matt Taylor scored a similar stunner just over 12 months earlier (October 2005). Who was it against?

4. At which London club was Harry Redknapp manager before his first tenure at Fratton Park?

5. Who holds the record for the most appearances for Portsmouth?

6. Who was the Pompey captain before Dejan Stefanovic?

7. Who did Pompey beat to win the FA Cup in 1939?

8. And who was captain of the title-winning side?

9. In which year did Pompey win promotion to the Premiership?

10. With which team did Pedro Mendes win the Champions League?

Answers on page 60

Top Ten Goals 2006/07

There were some truly fantastic goals during the 2006/07 season. Some of them were spectacular jaw droppers whilst others were simply the result of sheer flashes of brilliance. These are our top ten stunners...

Kanu V Middlesbrough (A), 28 August 2006

Pompey were leading comfortably by 2-0, when Kanu's superb solo effort gave the side a third goal. The Nigerian striker expertly controlled the ball in the centre of the pitch and then waltzed down half the length of the field before calmly slotting the ball past Schwarzer to complete his brace.

Pedro Mendes V Reading (H), 28 October 2006

It was a typical Pedro Mendes strike which sealed Portsmouth's 3-1 victory over Premier League new boys Reading. Matthew Taylor's corner, from the right, was cleared from the edge of the area and to the waiting Portuguese midfielder. He volleyed home a goal which was reminiscent of the trio of long-range efforts he had scored for Pompey during the 2005/06 season.

Kanu V Watford (H), 18 November 2006

After the shock of finding themselves trailing 1-0 to Watford, Kanu grabbed an equaliser for Portsmouth just before half-time. David Thompson had put in a good cross from the right, which found the striker. However, Foster saved his initial shot but Sean Davis slid in to prevent the ball from being cleared and Kanu coolly lifted the ball over the keeper.

(Pictured right)

Matthew Taylor V Everton (H), 9 December 2006

Taylor gave Portsmouth the lead with what would be the club's goal of the season, when he stunned Fratton Park with this wonder strike. Kanu and Everton's Simon Davies both scrambled for the same ball and it bobbled up for Taylor, who then unleashed a phenomenal volley from 45 yards. Howard was helpless as it dipped past him and into the goal.

(Pictured right)

Kanu V Everton (H), 9 December 2006

Minutes after Taylor's effort, Kanu extended Pompey's lead with a fantastic volley. He had connected with a cross from Gary O'Neil to launch the ball past Howard and into the bottom corner.

Matthew Taylor V Arsenal (A), 16 December 2006

Seven days after his wonder goal against Everton, Matthew Taylor once again stunned onlookers with another effort to double Pompey's lead shortly after half time. Thompson's attempt on goal was cleared and fell to Taylor who hammered home a left-footed volley from the edge of the area.

Pedro Mendes V Manchester City (H), 10 February 2007

Portsmouth took an early lead when Pedro Mendes fired one of his seemingly regulation volleys into the back of Manchester City's net. Andreas Isaksson met a Matthew Taylor corner, however he could only clear it as far as Mendes. His first touch cleverly misled Ousamane Dabo before he curled home the fantastic strike with the outside of his left foot - a move that would remind fans of his double against the same opposition last season.

(Pictured left)

Niko Kranjcar V Fulham (A), 31 March 2007

The Croatian midfielder gave Portsmouth the lead in the opening minutes of the game with a superb effort from just outside the area. Kanu flicked the ball and Kranjcar duly collected the ball to surprise Fulham with a brilliantly taken strike which soared into the top corner of Niemi's net. (Pictured right)

Arnold Mvuemba V Watford (A), 9 April 2007   (Pictured above)

After coming on as a substitute in the 80th minute, Mvuemba found himself on the score sheet in less than sixty seconds. O'Neil managed to find some space to provide a cross for the midfielder, who then sent home a classy volley. It was a fine debut goal, despite the eventual result.

Matthew Taylor V Newcastle (H), 14 April 2007

Matthew Taylor once again sent home a stunning goal to seal another Pompey victory. On the 59th minute the midfielder latched onto the ball around 30 yards out and thumped an awesome strike straight into the bottom left corner of the goal, much to the joy of an erupting Fratton Park. (Pictured right)

Frogmore

Who Said That?

Can you match the following quotes to the player who spoke them?

1 "I think it's a new start for Portsmouth so fortunately I didn't save Mendes' goals last season!"

☐ A Djimi Traoré

2 "The chant about me - 'you'll never get your haircut' - I thought was funny"

☐ B Matthew Taylor

3 "It was a good goal but you have to remember that Kanu's was a fantastic goal as well."

☐ C Richard Hughes

4 "I think boxing has helped me as a footballer."

☐ D Lomana LuaLua

5 "When I was younger I was running around and I crashed into a wall. I was playing with my brother and I didn't see the wall ahead of me!"

☐ E Sean Davis

6 "The fans in Portsmouth have been fantastic to me. In my career I never thought I would go through such a period without a goal, but they stayed behind me and I am very grateful."

☐ F Linvoy Pimus

7 "I enjoyed cooking a lot more before I lost the cook-off to Jamo!"

☐ G Niko Kranjcar

8 "The team are all wonderful guys. They have made me feel very welcome."

☐ H David James

9 "I guess my brother Kazenga takes after me that way, but I should probably tell him to cut the somersaults out before he gets himself injured!"

☐ I Benjani Mwaruwari

10

"The only way we can make this happen is to dream big, so that's what we are doing."

☐ J Lauren

Write the number next to the name of the player and turn to page 61 to find out if you are correct.

29

David James

Goalkeeper David James enjoyed a phenomenal first season at Portsmouth in 2006/07, which saw him break the Premier League clean sheet record, previously held by David Seaman. However, the England international is self-effacing about his achievement.

"The record was nice. I keep saying it - and it may sound selfish - but it was an achievement that has been over my entire career and not one season. But it was also the 11th clean sheet of the season, which in itself broke Portsmouth's record I'm told, so that's an achievement that I'm proud about," he shrugged, before going on to talk about the season as a whole.

"The season was terrific, the start especially. I think up until November/December we were in the top six. Things were good for us, although perhaps the frustrating thing was the away form. But the home form had been so good that it pulled us through.

"As I say the home form was great, but the away form has been disappointing. I think we had three wins so there is a lot of room for improvement. In some respects we sort of polarised in terms of results although not performance. So we finished where we should have finished. If we had doubled our away wins, that would have been another nine points and that would have put us straight into Europe. I think if there's disappointment, then it is that we went to Everton and lost 3-0. It was 0-0 at half time, we could have and should have held them but their victory put them into Europe."

Despite the disappointment of missing out on a place in Europe, Jamo - as he is nicknamed - said he had thoroughly enjoyed his inaugural year at Fratton Park. "The season as a whole was great, the fans were fantastic and what with the European tour songs, Gary O'Neil's haircut, the announcement of the new stadium - everything that went alongside it was brilliant.

"I could try to pick out a few highlights, but the truth is that the season as a whole was a highlight. As a team we won, lost and drew together and no matter what the result - be it ecstatic after beating Manchester United or dire after losing 3-0 to Blackburn

- everything was done as a team. It's easy sometimes to win a game and for one man to go off and say 'well it was all me, everyone else just facilitates me because I'm super', just as when something goes wrong it can all be blamed on one person because he did something wrong but it hasn't been like that here. When we went through the bleak New Year we kept together, a lot of teams can break apart but we didn't and that has been very important. So for me the fact that everyone gets on so well has been a highlight."

David was universally voted player of the season for Portsmouth. Whilst he is clearly still delighted to have received the recognition, he is also refreshingly modest about his awards. "Getting voted Player of the Season by the fans and by the players was massive. It means a lot to me and those awards have taken pride of place in my kitchen, but you look at it and think well there's Matty, there's Linvoy, Sol and a host of other players who could have and should have had the same reward, so it's nice but it's not just about me. It's about the team and it is the team that puts you in the position to be able to receive any recognition."

> "As a team we won, lost and drew together and no matter what the result … everything was done as a team."

Player Profiles

Sol Campbell

Position: Defence

Born: 18 September 1974

Nationality: English

Pompey Debut: 19 August 2006 v Blackburn (H)

Previous Clubs: Tottenham, Arsenal

It can be no fluke that Portsmouth's most successful season in more than 50 years coincided with the arrival of the iconic England defender Sol Campbell. The defender has been the rock at the heart of Pompey's back four and has been instrumental in the performances that saw the side soar up the league table.

Campbell joined Pompey in August 2006, after bringing the curtain down on his five years at Arsenal. He enjoyed a triumphant period with the Gunners. With them he won two league titles and the FA Cup, after moving to Highbury from Tottenham. His last contribution for Arsenal was to score in the Champions League Final, proving that he was ready for his third World Cup with England in Germany.

Djimi Traoré

Position: Defence

Born: 1 March 1980

Nationality: Malian

Pompey Debut: 13 January 2007 v Sheffield United (A)

Previous Clubs: Charlton, Liverpool

The Mali international arrived at Fratton Park in January 2007, after spending the first half of the season at Charlton Athletic.

Prior to that Traoré had enjoyed a successful period at Liverpool, for whom he made more than 160 appearances. During his time at Anfield, he won the Champions League in dramatic style in 2005, the FA Cup in 2006 and the League Cup in 2003.

A tall and versatile defender, Djimi appears to have settled into life on the south coast.

Sean Davis

Position: Midfield

Born: 20 September 1979

Nationality: English

Pompey Debut: 14 January 2006 v Everton (H)

Previous Clubs: Tottenham, Fulham

Sean Davis began his career at Fulham, shining for the club at youth level before making his first team debut in 1996, aged 17. He proved to be a rising talent and was soon named England U21 captain.

His performances for the Craven Cottage side continued to improve, year on year and he became a key player in their rise through the leagues culminating in promotion to the Premier League. Davis was also sparking interest from several other top flight clubs and in July 2004 he made the short move across the capital to White Hart Lane.

However, injury troubles restricted his chances at Tottenham and when he returned to fitness he struggled to find his way back into the first team, which prompted his transfer to Portsmouth in 2006. Since then he has put in consistently high performances in midfield. And with a reputation of being a bit of a prankster, he has proved to be a character off the pitch.

Richard Hughes

Position: Midfield

Born: 25 June 1979

Nationality: Scottish

Pompey Debut: 13 August 2002 v Sheffield United (A)

Previous Clubs: Grimsby (loan), Bournemouth, Arsenal, Atalanta

A cultured and determined Scot, Hughes was born in Glasgow but moved to Milan whilst still a baby. He learned his trade at Atalanta before coming to the attention of Arsenal who snapped him up when he was 18. After a year in the Gunners' reserves, he moved to Bournemouth.

It was there that his tenacity in midfield drew the gaze of Harry Redknapp who signed him in 2002. Richard began his Portsmouth career well, but lost his place after injury and ended the season on loan at Grimsby. Since then Hughes has learned that patience and hard work reaps its own reward.

David James

Position:	Goalkeeper
Born:	1 August 1970
Nationality:	English
Pompey Debut:	19 August 2006 v Blackburn (H)
Previous Clubs:	Manchester City, West Ham, Aston Villa, Liverpool, Watford

After joining Portsmouth in 2006, David James had an impressive first season on the south coast. Five consecutive clean sheets at the beginning of the campaign would set the tone for the year for the highly rated 'keeper.

Consistently high performances and a series of spectacular saves saw James surpass the Premier League clean sheet record, as well as spark renewed calls for the shot stopper to return to the England set-up.

James began his career at Watford, progressing through the youth system at Vicarage Road. From there he was snapped up by Liverpool in 1992. Two years later, he made his full England debut in a friendly against Mexico.

Kanu

Position:	Forward
Born:	1 August 1976
Nationality:	Nigerian
Pompey Debut:	19 August 2006 v Blackburn (H)
Previous Clubs:	West Bromwich Albion, Arsenal, Inter Milan, Ajax

When Kanu joined Portsmouth in 2006, it would be fair to say some eyebrows were raised. He had spent two years at West Bromwich Albion, where he had struggled to settle, scoring just a handful of goals. However, the Nigerian international silenced his doubters with four goals in as many games at the start of the 2006/07 season. Just beyond the half-way point Kanu's haul had exceeded the total that had been racked up at his previous side.

It shouldn't have come as a surprise. Prior to West Brom, Kanu spent several seasons at Arsenal where he proved himself to be a top striker notching up 44 goals in 197 appearances. What is even more incredible is that in 1996 a routine medical at Inter Milan revealed a serious heart defect, which could have ended his career. However, such is Kanu's determination he recovered from surgery and came back seemingly stronger than ever.

During his career the player has won numerous honours, including the Champions League with Ajax and Olympic Gold for Nigeria in Atlanta. He has also been named African Footballer of the Year twice.

Niko Kranjcar

Position:	Midfield
Born:	13 August 1984
Nationality:	Croatian
Pompey Debut:	19 September 2006 v Mansfield Town (A)
Previous Clubs:	Hajduk Split, Dinamo Zagreb

Niko Kranjcar has been hailed as being 'the greatest promise of Croatian football'. He began his career with Dinamo Zagreb, as part of their youth system, but his ability saw him rapidly ascend to make his senior debut at just 16. His meteoric rise saw him not only cement a regular spot, but also reap the reward of becoming captain whilst still in his teens. In his first year as skipper he led the team to a league and super cup double.

However in January 2005, he made the shock move to Dinamo's big rival Hajduk Split, where he added another championship medal to his collection. His performances led to international recognition and he shone for Croatia during the 2006 World Cup, attracting the attentions of numerous European clubs.

In his first year at Portsmouth he proved himself to have a bright future, with a number of impressive showings not to mention his stylish debut goal against Fulham in April.

Lauren

Position:	Midfield/Defence
Born:	19 January 1977
Nationality:	Cameroonian
Pompey Debut:	20 January 2007 v Charlton (H)
Previous Clubs:	Arsenal, RCD Mallorca, Levante, Seville B

The former Cameroon international began his career in Spain, playing for Sevilla, Levante and then RCD Mallorca before he made the switch to Arsenal in 2000. That same year also saw the player pick up an Olympic Gold medal for Cameroon in Sydney.

He thrived as an attacking right back and won several honours with the Gunners, including twice lifting the league title. Lauren was a key member of Arsenal's team when he picked up a serious knee injury in January 2006, which kept him on the sidelines for almost a year. When he was fit to return, Lauren found it difficult to push his way back into the first team and made the decision to join Portsmouth in January 2007.

Since then his experience and talent has proved to be invaluable for the Pompey squad.

Lomana Tresor LuaLua

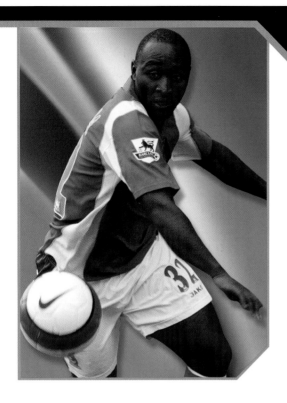

Position:	Forward
Born:	28 December 1980
Nationality:	Congolese
Pompey Debut:	7 February 2004 v Tottenham (A)
Previous Clubs:	Newcastle, Colchester

A speedy frontman with amazing natural flair, LuaLua first proved his worth on loan at Fratton Park in February 2004, before making the move permanent the following summer.

He began his career at Colchester, before his skills attracted the attention of Newcastle. He moved to St James' Park in 2000, where he was primarily used as a substitute. LuaLua grew frustrated and he jumped at the chance to play first team football with Portsmouth.

He quickly won the affection of the supporters with his spectacular celebrations. However 2006/07 was perhaps a disappointing season for the DR Congo captain, with injuries keeping him out of the squad for a large portion of the year.

Pedro Mendes

Position:	Midfield
Born:	26 February 1979
Nationality:	Portuguese
Pompey Debut:	14 January 2006 v Everton (H)
Previous Clubs:	Tottenham, FC Porto, Vitoria Guimaraes, FC Felgueira

Since his arrival on the south coast in January 2006, Pedro Mendes has become something of a cult hero, largely due to spectacular volleys and for scoring the goals that sparked Pompey's 'Great Escape' in 2005/06.

The Portuguese midfielder began his career at FC Felgueira before joining Vitoria Guimaraes. There he helped the side to lift the Portuguese Super Cup (in 2002/03). His performances attracted the attention of Jose Mourinho who snapped him up for FC Porto in July 2003.

Mendes played a key part in helping Porto to the Portuguese title, Cup and Champions League. A move to Spurs followed in 2004, where he perhaps became most famous for scoring the spectacular 'goal that wasn't' against Manchester United. However, Mendes struggled to settle at Tottenham. Since joining Portsmouth he has continued to demonstrate that he is adept at shooting at range, with all of his goals proving to be memorable.

Gary O'Neil

Position:	Midfield
Born:	18 May 1983
Nationality:	English
Pompey Debut:	29 January 2000 v Barnsley (H)
Previous Clubs:	Cardiff (loan), Walsall (loan)

One of the youngest members of the squad, O'Neil is also the longest serving Portsmouth player, having risen through the youth ranks at Fratton Park. He made his debut for the first team in 2000 aged just 16, looking like a 'cheeky ballboy', as one match reporter described.

Something of a fringe player in those early days, it has really been over the past three seasons that O'Neil has come into his own holding down a first team place that his status as England U21 captain had suggested he deserved.

In 2005/06 he grabbed headlines with consistently impressive performance, not to mention his seven goals. Although he was not as prominent on the score sheet last season, his stature in midfield has continued to grow and improve. All of these factors contributed to O'Neil becoming a natural choice to deputise as skipper in the absence of Dejan Stefanovic over the past two campaigns.

Benjani Mwaruwari

Position:	Forward
Born:	13 August 1978
Nationality:	Zimbabwean
Pompey Debut:	14 January 2006 v Everton (H)
Previous Clubs:	Auxerre, Grasshoppers Zurich, Jomo Cosmos

Benjani Mwaruwari joined Portsmouth in January 2006 for £4million (then a club record) and he has become somewhat of a fan favourite, due to his fantastic work rate and cheery disposition. Although he has not been a prolific goalscorer since his arrival, he has regularly played provider for his team-mates and his dedication is inspirational.

Voted South African Player of the Year in 2001, whilst playing for Jomo Cosmos, Benjani came to the attention of Grasshoppers Zurich. However, after just a season with them he was snapped up by Auxerre, whom he helped to French Cup glory in 2003 and 2004. However, the Zimbabwe captain never really settled in France and he jumped at the chance to try his hand in the Premier League with Pompey.

Noé Pamarot

Position:	Defence
Born:	14 April 1979
Nationality:	French
Pompey Debut:	14 January 2006 v Everton (H)
Previous Clubs:	Tottenham, Portsmouth (loan), Nice, Martigues, Paris FC

Pamarot first enjoyed a loan spell at Fratton Park in the late 90s. Noé began his career at Paris FC before moving to Nice, where his pace and strength in defence was impressive.

After five years in Ligue 1, the Frenchman joined Tottenham for £1.7million. For Pamarot it was a realisation of his ambition. However, after a promising start at White Hart Lane Noé's first-team action came to an abrupt halt when he tore ligaments in his knee. On returning to fitness, the defender struggled to get back into the first team and Harry Redknapp moved to bring him to Fratton Park in January 2006.

Since then Pamarot has proved to be a patient and solid squad player with versatility to play on either side of defence, despite a natural preference for the central positions.

Linvoy Primus

Position:	Defence
Born:	14 September 1973
Nationality:	English
Pompey Debut:	12 August 2000 v Sheffield United (A)
Previous Clubs:	Reading, Barnet, Charlton

One of Pompey's most reliable and popular players, Primus has seemingly come into his own since linking up with Sol Campbell in the heart of defence.

Since joining Portsmouth in 2000, the big-hearted defender has made a point of disproving and confounding his critics by setting a consistently high standard in his performances. Primus' dedication to his team has continued to set a glowing example to the other members of the squad and the most recent campaign has proved to be no exception.

This enthusiasm extends beyond the pitch, as Linvoy is one of Pompey's most active players when it comes to community and charity work. Alongside former Fratton favourites Darren Moore and Mick Mellows, he has set up his own charity, Faith and Football.

Dejan Stefanovic

Position:	Defence
Born:	28 October 1974
Nationality:	Serbian
Pompey Debut:	16 August 2003 v Aston Villa (H)
Previous Clubs:	Vitesse Arnhem, OFK Belgrade, Perugia, Sheffield Wednesday, Red Star Belgrade

Club Captain Dejan Stefanovic leads by example as one of the club's most consistent performers, in addition to being one of the team's most dedicated players.

He began his career at Red Star Belgrade before joining Sheffield United in 1995, then in the top flight. Three years in Holland followed before the defender made a return to England with Portsmouth in 2003.

Cultured yet uncompromising, Stefanovic prefers to play on the left side of central defence. However in 2006/07 he proved his flexibility by operating on the outside with little difficulty.

The last two seasons have been difficult for Dejan, who has spent portions of time playing through the pain barrier (with an ankle and then knee injury) before eventually succumbing to surgery. Both times he has worked hard to return to action sooner than expected, with little effect on his form.

Matthew Taylor

Position:	Midfield/Defence
Born:	27 November 1981
Nationality:	English
Pompey Debut:	10 August 2002 v Nottingham Forest (H)
Previous Clubs:	Luton

Matthew Taylor has begun to attract a reputation for scoring stunning goals following a number of spectacular strikes over the past two seasons, most notably his long-range efforts against Everton and Sunderland (in December 2006 and October 2005 respectively). However there is much more to the player than that.

Taylor appears to be equally as comfortable in midfield as he is in the back four. Since joining Portsmouth in 2002 his talent and hard work have seen the player become a key member of the squad. Over the past twelve months, continually improving performances have also led to calls for Matt to receive his first England call-up. It is surely only a matter of time before his efforts are rewarded.

Jamie Ashdown

Position:	Goalkeeper
Born:	20 November 1980
Nationality:	English
Pompey Debut:	21 September 2004 v Tranmere (A)
Previous Clubs:	Norwich (loan), Reading, Rushden & Diamonds (loan), Bournemouth (loan), Gravesend (loan)

The Reading-born shot stopper rose though the Royals' youth ranks before gaining valuable first-team experience during loan spells with Gravesend, Bournemouth and Rushden & Diamonds. His consistently high performances attracted the attentions of a number of top-flight clubs, but in June 2004 the former England Schoolboy opted to join Portsmouth.

Jamie spent much of 2005/06 as Pompey's first choice goalkeeper until first the arrival of Dean Kiely in January and then David James in the summer. However, he has continued to train hard as he patiently waits for his chance to shine. His ability and sheer determination indicates the young 'keeper has a bright future ahead of him.

John Utaka

Summer Signing

Position: Forward

Born: 8 January 1982

Nationality: Nigerian

Previous Clubs: Rennes, Lens, Al-Sadd, Ismaily SC

Nigeria international Utaka joined Pompey in the summer from French top-flight side Rennes, where the 25-year-old operated as both a striker and a wide player.

After starting his career in Egypt with Al Ismaili, Utaka moved to Qatar to play for Al Sadd. From there he moved to Europe and enjoyed a successful three-year spell with French club Lens, before signing for Rennes in 2005.

In his two years there, Utaka scored 22 goals in 62 appearances. He hit the headlines last February when he netted consecutive hat-tricks against his former club Lens and Lyon.

David Nugent

Position: Forward

Born: 2 May 1985

Nationality: English

Previous Clubs: Preston North End, Bury

David Nugent arrived at Portsmouth in July 2007, after leaving Preston North End to make the step up to top flight action.

The young striker was frequently on target for the Championship side, scoring 33 goals in 94 appearances.

His goalscoring exploits attracted the attention of Steve McClaren, who handed the player his first cap in March 2007 and in doing so Nugent became the first Preston player to play for England since Sir Tom Finney in 1958.

David made an instant impact, when, after coming on as a late substitute he scored to cement a 3-0 victory over Andorra.

Summer Signing

Hermann Hreidarsson

Position: Defence

Born: 11 July 1974

Nationality: Icelandic

Previous Clubs: Charlton, Ipswich, Wimbledon, Brentford, Crystal Palace, IBV

After leaving Charlton in June 2007, Hermann Hreidarsson made the short move to the south coast.

During his four year tenure with the Addicks, the Iceland international made more than 150 appearances for the club and impressed fans and experts alike with his commanding displays in defence.

Hreidarsson first came to England in 1997, when he joined Crystal Palace. Spells at Brentford, Wimbledon and Ipswich followed before his move to Charlton.

A versatile defender, Hermann is able to play at left back or in the centre of defence.

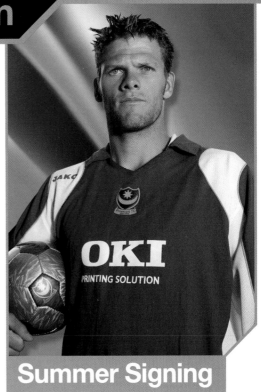

Summer Signing

Sulley Muntari

Summer Signing

Position:	Midfield
Born:	27 August 1984
Nationality:	Ghanaian
Previous Clubs:	Udinese

A talented midfielder, Sulley Muntari became Pompey's record signing over the summer.

Harry Redknapp had been following the Ghana international for months, before finally capturing his man in June 2007.

He joined Pompey from Udinese, where he had been impressing spectators of the Serie A team for the past few seasons with a strong performances in the heart of midfield, not to mention making a big impact on the international stage.

Muntari is a key player in the Ghana team and has scored 8 goals from 26 appearances for his country.

Described by Football Italia as possessing "the touch of Kaka and the combativeness of Edgar Davids", the young African's star looks set to soar.

Sylvain Distin

Position:	Defence
Born:	16 December 1977
Nationality:	French
Previous Clubs:	Manchester City, Newcastle (loan), Paris St Germain, Tours

Perhaps one of the best players never to have received international recognition, Sylvain Distin arrived at Portsmouth in June with a string of plaudits to his name.

The highly-rated defender joined the south coast side from Manchester City, where he had been a formidable rock at the heart of the Mancunian side's line for the past five years.

During his time at the north-west team, Distin proved to be a model of consistency – both in terms of performance and availability.

Tall and agile with a good turn of pace, the defender looks set to continue in the same vein for Portsmouth.

Summer Signing

Spot the
difference

Hidden in the second picture are six changes. Can you find them all?

1

2

Answers on page 60

Linvoy Primus

Linvoy Primus is a disappointed man. Not because he has missed out on an award but because he was unable to take part in a Faith and Football organised charity trek in Mount Sinai.

The defender had been gearing up for the challenge in Egypt, but had to pull out to undergo surgery. "I was really disappointed that I couldn't go, but I am proud of the guys who went out there.

"It was tough, we knew it was going to be hard, but they have raised a lot of money and it will be put to good use – believe me!" he said.

This challenge is the second of this type to be organised by Faith and Football, the first being a walk along part of the Great Wall of China in 2005. These came about when Linvoy and the other members of the organisation visited poverty stricken areas in Nigeria and India. After witnessing the reality of the situation in these countries, they realised they wanted to do more to help support the need for orphanages and schools - not just by providing a one-off cash injection but by supplying continual funding. That's what the money raised from the trips to Egypt and China has and will be going towards assisting the charity's Christian Mission partners to help house, feed and educate children. "The first time I went to Nigeria, we played football with the kids, we coached them a bit and we talked to them. For some of these children, they couldn't understand why a man from England would want to go out there and spend time with them.

"Since leaving we have continued to get regular updates and those children have gone on to help other kids who are younger than them. When you hear that, you realise how much you can influence somebody's life by just spending a little bit of time with them."

Linvoy isn't the only player in the Pompey squad to be giving up his time to give back to those less fortunate than himself. David James, Lomana LuaLua and Kanu have all got their own foundations and the big-hearted player is not surprised, revealing that he believes it is important for footballers to use their positions wisely.

"I think for us to be able to give something back, no matter how big or how small, we have to try. We've been blessed with talent and the opportunity to use it, so we should use that to help others. For those who are doing something, I think it is great because they are changing lives.

"In life, there aren't many role models around and the ones that are there can sometimes get lost in what the world is doing. But if there are role models within a sport that is globally accepted then why not use that to help influence and then change people's lives? You aren't in this game for long so you have to take and then make the most of those opportunities."

> "… you realise how much you can influence somebody's life by just spending a little bit of time with them."

Crossword Quiz

Can you find the answers to complete the crossword?

Answers on page 61

Across

1. (See also 11 across) The name of the ground where Pompey play (7,4)

6. Noé Pamarot scored his first goal for Portsmouth against this team (7)

7. Pompey's Croatian midfielder. Niko ___ (8)

8. Pompey's first opposition of the 2007/08 season (5)

11. See 1 across (7,4)

12. See 3 down (9,7)

13. Pompey had their biggest win of the 2006/07 season against this North-East team (13)

15. The top scorer for Pompey in 2006/07 (4)

16. Pompey defender. Dejan ___ (10)

Down

2. See 5 down (5,8)

3. (See also 12 across) The Bulgarian striker who was Pompey's top scorer when the team won promotion to the Premier League (9,7)

4. This London team will provide Pompey's opposition for the final game of the 2007/08 season?

5. (See also 2 down) The Pompey manager (5,8)

9. The Pompey mascot (8)

10. Pedro Mendes is a native of this European country (8)

14. This Pompey defender used to play for 6 across. ___ Campbell (3)

Did You Know?

- Goalkeeper David James once trained with NFL side Miami Dolphins

- Sol Campbell is the first England player to have played in six consecutive major tournaments

- Defensive rock Linvoy Primus' nickname is Predator

- Djimi Traoré has a scar on his forehead. He got it when he ran into a wall when he was younger

- Lauren enjoys boxing in his spare time

- Matthew Taylor is a patron of the RSPCA

- Scottish midfielder Richard Hughes is terrified of snakes

- Both David James and Jamie Ashdown are keen artists

- Both Lauren and Kanu are Olympic gold medallists with Cameroon (2000) and Nigeria (1996) respectively.

- Whilst playing for Cameroon Lauren competed alongside goalkeeper Jacques Songo'o, father of Pompey's Franck Songo'o

- Matt Taylor admits that his worst habits are hogging the television remote and watching too much football!

A FEW OF OUR FAVOURITE THINGS...

The Pompey players reveal a few of their favourite things in life...

MY FAVOURITE ICE CREAM FLAVOUR IS... **Vanilla** - Niko Kranjcar, **Praline and Cream** - Noé Pamarot, **Cookie Dough** - Richard Hughes, **Vanilla** - Benjani.

MY FAVOURITE CARTOON CHARACTER IS... **Goofy** - Pedro Mendes, **Roadrunner** - Jamie Ashdown.

MY FAVOURITE SPORTS PERSON IS ... **Tiger Woods** - Gary O'Neil, **Michael Jordan** - Linvoy Primus, **Mohammad Ali** - Kanu.

Sol Campbell

Scrambled Up

Can you rearrange the words below to find the players' names?

1	SPY VIOLIN RUM	
2	ISLAND TINS IVY	
3	MENDED ROPES	
4	UNREAL	
5	JAM ADVISED	
6	NINJA ROCK ARK	
7	SURLY MEAL UNIT	
8	DIRE JAM TRIO	
9	MANDARINS SHORN HERE	
10	JET INFO ADVANCES	

Answers on page 61

Super
Matty Taylor

When Everton visited Fratton Park last season, the stands rocked to thunderous renditions of 'Super Matty Taylor' after the Pompey star sensationally scored a spectacular goal past Tim Howard from 45 yards out.

It is perhaps one of the most memorable moments from a year which itself will linger in the mind as Pompey's most successful for more than 50 years.

Looking back at the 2006/07 campaign, Matthew Taylor said he was delighted by the team's achievement.

"It's been a fantastic season, we've had some good results at Fratton Park but maybe we have suffered a little bit away from home, which is something we need to improve on.

"I haven't got too many complaints personally. I've played consistently, had a very good run in the team and I scored nine goals, which is fantastic. I would have liked to have got up to ten, but I think you always want to do better. Overall though, I think Portsmouth had a pleasing season, certainly the best one in the Premiership."

His effort against Everton was deservedly voted Pompey goal of the season by supporters, however Taylor's reaction to his award is typically modest.

accolades. It was a goal that helped the team and that's the important thing. We play as a team and that means we win together and we celebrate together, regardless as to goalscorers. That's what being in a team is about, any result is down to the team as a whole. It's a cliché but we can't do anything if we play as individuals."

Looking ahead to the future, Matt was excited to see the plans for the new stadium. However he admits that looking at the proposals, there was a slight bittersweet feeling as it will spell the end of Pompey's long history at Fratton Park. "The club is progressing and improving on and off the pitch, which speaks volumes about where the owner wants the club to be. That can only be good for the team.

"The new stadium looks fantastic - it shows exactly how far the club has moved forward. I think the only thing is that it will be sad to leave Fratton Park. I think the important thing when we get to the stadium is to make sure the atmosphere remains just as good. A lot of people talk about a lack of atmosphere at new grounds, but I'm sure that won't be the case because Pompey fans are so passionate. As I say it will be a sad day when we leave Fratton Park, but it is also exciting that we will be moving to a state-of-the-art stadium."

"It was obviously wonderful to see the goal go in. I didn't think I had scored the goal of the season for Portsmouth to be honest and of course I am delighted with that, but for me it's not about picking up personal

> " ...we win together and we celebrate together, regardless as to goalscorers."

A Few Firsts

The Pompey players reveal some of their firsts...

My Childhood Football Idol Was...

Glenn Hoddle
Matt Taylor

Paul 'Gazza' Gasgoine
Gary O'Neil

Pele
Lomana LuaLua

My First Football Shirt Was...

Tottenham Hotspur
Linvoy Primus

Liverpool
Jamie Ashdown

As A Child I Supported...

AC Milan
Dejan Stefanovic

Paris Saint Germain
Djimi Traoré

My First Car Was...

A red Nissan Micra
Matt Taylor

A Vauxhall Tigra
Gary O'Neil

A Volkswagen Golf
Linvoy Primus

A Ford Sierra
Richard Hughes

My First CD/Album Was...

**Gangsta's Paradise
by Coolio**
Jamie Ashdown

**Sultans of Swing
by Dire Straits**
Richard Hughes

Can you guess who these players are?

Unscramble the picture and see if you are correct by turning to page 60.

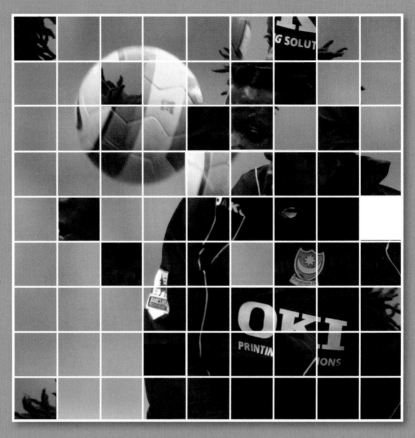

Wordsearch

See if you can find the former Pompey players in the wordsearch below…

```
D I C F I M A H G N I T T I H W N S O N
R E I D F A M E R S A M A W F S S E G E
J R E N R H A R R I S S S A E N A C K L
E I S I A G K C E L A P D A W P D E R A
J A D E T N A N W Q U I N Q C F H E S T
E L N R M I C K A G L L P E H M O N F P
S I U D T R P E F R A L T T O N R R N T
A H T U Y E R A L K N I T I U P O R D E
T S K D O H M O S G U H C A T H F E L D
A L A N N S I F C I A P A U L J A U T D
G U C N U S E W R E F E N E E E C P U Y
N P A A S T H I N O R T H I E C N I V L
R E N L R E C N A D G A G E G N K E R F
P E T E R N W C E T O G T B E S L R N K
T O E R S N H I H S U R A I K R E N N R
E A S O O G M O N D G I F T B E S I I S
R E N S R O S R Y N M P K R T O G B U E
O U R S T R G U Y H O C O R N H S A Q A
O E E E N F A E M P A E S A T N M A A T
M T J L O Y M M I J R D I C K I N S O N
```

Andy	Peter	Paul	Duggie
Awford	**Harris**	**Merson**	**Reid**
Jimmy	Vince	Mick	Teddy
Dickinson	**Hilaire**	**Quinn**	**Sheringham**
Jack	Alan	Len	Guy
Froggatt	**Knight**	**Phillips**	**Whittingham**

Answers on page 61

Where In The World?

Once upon a time, Pompey's players were predominantly English, with a smattering of Scottish and Welsh players thrown in. Nowadays, with the Premier League being a global industry, Portsmouth has attracted players from far and wide – although it still has a large contingent of English stars. This map shows where in the world some of the players have come from to play football at Fratton Park...

1 Portugal
Pedro Mendes

2 Croatia
Niko Kranjcar

3 France
Sylvain Distin

4 Serbia
Dejan Stefanovic

5 Iceland
Hermann Hreidarsson

6 Nigeria
Kanu

7 Cameroon
Lauren

8 Ghana
Sulley Muntari

9 DR Congo
Lomana LuaLua

10 Zimbabwe
Benjani Marwari

11 Mali
Djimi Traoré

Pompey's State-of-the-Art New Stadium Plans

In April 2007, Portsmouth revealed plans for a spectacular new football stadium, which will be built on reclaimed land in the city's dockyard.

The ground has been designed by leading architects Herzog and de Meuron, who were responsible for both the Allianz Stadium in Munich and the Beijing National Stadium, which will be the centrepiece of the 2008 Olympic Games.

This stunning ground is planned to be located on a site adjacent to the historic Naval Dockyards, the Gunwharf Quays retail and leisure centre, Portsmouth Harbour station and ferry terminus and the Hard interchange bus station – giving it excellent links to public transport.

Planning applications for the proposed development are due to be submitted by the end of the year, following consultation with stakeholders and, subject to the necessary consent, the reclamation work could get underway in summer 2008 and the construction of the stadium the following year. It is anticipated that Pompey will be playing in their new home by 2011.

Answers

2006/2007 Season Quiz

1. Svetoslav Todorov
2. Niko Kranjcar
3. B) 12
4. Manchester City (Away), 23.08.06
5. Hajduk Split
6. Wigan Athletic
7. Kanu
8. 12
9. Noe Pamarot
10. 142
11. A) 12
12. 9th

The Pompey Quiz

1. A) 1898
2. Sherlock Holmes
3. Sunderland
4. West Ham United
5. Jimmy Dickinson
6. Arjan de Zeeuw
7. Wolverhampton Wanderers
8. Jimmy Guthrie
9. 2003
10. Porto

Guess Who?

Benjani Mwaruwari

Gary O'Neil

Spot the difference

Wordsearch

```
D I C F I M A H G N I T T I H W N S O N
R E I D F A M E R S A M A W F S S E G E
J R E N R H A R R I S S S A E N A C K L
E I S I A G K C E L A P D A W P D E R A
J A D E T N A N W Q U I N Q C F H E S T
E L N R M I C K A G L L P E H M O N F P
S I U D T R P E F R A L T T O N R R N T
A H T U Y E R A L K N I T I U P O R D E
T S K D O H M O S G U H C A T H F E L D
A L A N N S I F C I A P A U L J A U T D
G U C N U S E W R E F E N E E E C P U Y
N P A A S T H I N O R T H I E C N I V L
R E N L R E C N A D G A G E G N K E R F
P E T E R N W C E T O G T B E S L R N K
T O E R S N H I H S U R A I K R E N N R
E A S O O G M O N D G I F T B E S I I S
R E N S R O S R Y N M P K R T O G B U E
O U R S T R G U Y H O C O R N H S A Q A
O E E N F A E M P A E S A T N M A A T
M T J L O Y M M I J R D I C K I N S O N
```

Who Said That?

1.	H	6.	I
2.	E	7.	C
3.	B	8.	G
4.	J	9.	D
5.	A	10.	F

Scrambled Up

1.	Linvoy Primus	6.	Niko Kranjcar
2.	Sylvain Distin	7.	Sulley Muntari
3.	Pedro Mendes	8.	Djimi Traore
4.	Lauren	9.	Hermann Hreidarsson
5.	David James	10.	Dejan Stefanovic

Crossword Quiz

Across:
1. FRATTON
6. ARSENAL
7. KRANJCAR
8. DERBY
11. PARK
13. TODOROV
14. MIDDLESBROUGH
16. KANU
18. STEFANOVIC